A Practical Guide to

PATCHWORK

From the Victoria and Albert Museum

*Illus. 1: **Detail of patchwork cover** of printed and plain cottons, dated 1797. (Museum no. T.102–1938)*

A Practical Guide to

PATCHWORK

From the Victoria and Albert Museum

Edited, with an Introduction, by Linda Parry

THE MAIN STREET PRESS ● Pittstown, New Jersey

First American edition 1987

Published by
The Main Street Press, Inc.
William Case House
Pittstown, NJ 08867

Published originally by
Unwin Hyman
an imprint of Unwin Hyman Limited
London, England

Designed by Clare Clements
Technical instructions by Valerie Jackson
Illustrations by Jil Shipley
Technical adviser: Alyson Morris

Filmset by MS Filmsetting Limited, Frome,
Somerset
Printed in Great Britain by
Blantyre Printing & Binding Co. Ltd., London & Glasgow

Library of Congress Cataloging-in-Publication Data

Victoria and Albert Museum.
    A practical guide to patchwork from the Victoria and
Albert Museum.

    Bibliography: p.
    1. Patchwork—Patterns. 2. Victoria and Albert
Museum—Art collections.   I. Parry, Linda.   II. Title.
III. Title: Patchwork.
TT835.V53 1987   746.46   87–14163
ISBN 1–55562–032–9

CONTENTS

FOREWORD

The purpose of this series of books is to introduce particular sections of the embroidery collection of the Victoria and Albert Museum and to serve as a bridge between the two quite separate historical and technical approaches to the subject. Patterns will be provided of selected Museum objects embroidered in many different styles and techniques and it is hoped that the additional technical information will inspire many readers to embroider items themselves, just as the experienced craftsperson should find inspiration from learning more of the history of the craft. Thus, by studying each embroidery technique separately through examples from the Museum's collection, a re-assessment of historic embroidery and its applications to modern design will be possible.

INTRODUCTION

It is almost 50 years since the last Museum book concerning patchwork was published (*Notes on Applied Work and Patchwork*, HMSO, 1938). In the intervening years the collection has increased three-fold with the addition of 40 examples of the technique including significant early examples. This book, because of its technical format, is limited in its survey; the earliest and most recently worked pieces tend to be the most complicated from a technical viewpoint which has precluded their inclusion in the technical section. It is hoped, however, that the following survey will redress this imbalance by giving a more complete picture of the collection as a whole.

For the sake of purity and clarity, only items showing pieced or mosaic patchwork as their main technique have been included. Hopefully, the allied skills of quilting and appliqué will provide later subjects for this series. Names of patchwork patterns and shapes vary greatly from place to place and the titles adopted for the contents list have no historic importance or significance.

There are approximately 60 examples of patchwork in the Museum's collection. Although most take the form of bed covers, there are also a full set of 18th-century bed hangings, a number of small domestic items including a man's dressing gown from the 19th century and two examples of 20th-century *haute*

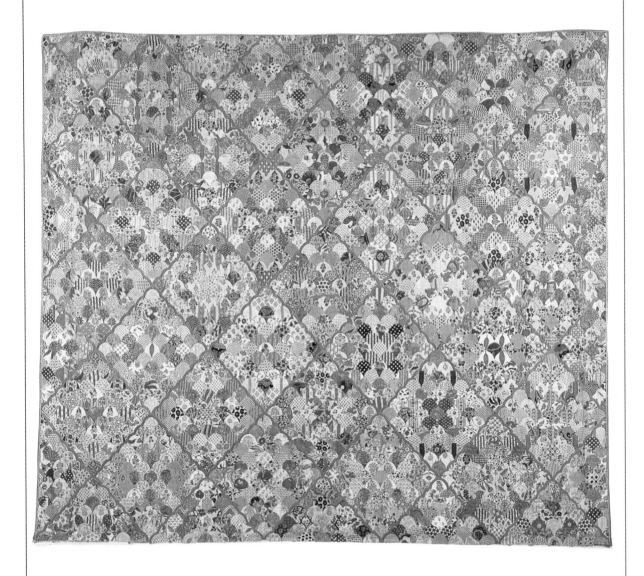

*Illus. 2: **Hanging from a set of bed hangings** Clam shell design worked in cottons, linens and fustians of European and Indian origin, about 1730. (Museum no. 242–1908)*

*Illus. 3: **Patchwork bed cover** of printed and plain cottons with some additional embroidery. The border shows various naval and military scenes, the central panel probably depicts George III reviewing volunteers, about 1805. (Museum no. T.9–1962)*

couture: two women's outfits designed in America by Adolpho in 1967 utilising earlier patchwork pieces. In addition to the classic pieced patchworks, some of the late 18th-century and early 19th-century bed covers employ mixed techniques of patchwork, appliqué and additional hand embroidery while two mid-19th-century hangings in the collection use pieced, applied and embroidered felts to achieve quite different effects.

The Museum does not attempt to collect every type of design and county variation of the craft, as to do so would duplicate other specialist collections. The collection has been formed, however, to reflect the skillful use of a decorative technique in a national rather than a local context. The four American examples in the collection illustrate both the development of British social traditions and some significant American developments since the late 18th century (pp. 62 and 66).

As part of the department which houses the national collection of textiles, the component parts of each patchwork (printed and painted cottons and linens, woven silks, braids and ribbons) are all considered as important, and in some instances more so, than the quilt composition itself. Allied items such as printed cotton quilt centres and templates are represented in the collection as well as an incomplete bed cover in various stages of assembly, which graphically illustrates the sewing elements involved. Such national events as Wellington's victory at Vittoria (*see* p. 30), the Jubilee of George III and Queen Victoria's Coronation are all commemorated on patchworks in the collection, as are the more personal and poignant details of marriages (also p. 30) and births (p. 18). Such historic details add interest to the quilts and help to date them more precisely, for only in a few examples has the maker added such details as her name and the year of completion. An assessment of the patterns of the silks and cottons is often necessary in the dating of such examples, as the patterns of patchwork change little from generation to generation. Most of the compositions of the Museum's examples are traditionally British, made up from formal repeating bands of hexagons, squares and diamonds. There are few examples in the collection of the more flamboyant two-tone designs which depend on strong repeating

shapes, an art practised in the North of England and now particularly associated with American work. One late example, of lemon and yellow cotton sateen and made in the Northumberland village of Backworth in about 1900, shows a simple framed star centre but this and the striped borders merely provide a subordinate background for the superb range of traditional quilting patterns worked overall.

Although pieced techniques can be found on much earlier examples of European furnishings, the Museum's earliest examples of British patchwork date from the 18th century. Two rare early silk bed covers are particularly interesting. One is made up in strips of patterned silk dress ribbons; and the other, a framed design, utilises plain and embroidered velvets and woven fabrics of silk and metal thread, many taken from the finest and most expensive of court dresses of the period 1690–1710. Both examples are likely to have been made by the families of drapers or dress makers because of the extensive range of fabrics used which exceed any one family's normal requirements, however rich or socially active. Also dating from the 18th century is a unique set of bed hangings and valances of clam-shell design, outlined with lime green silk ribbon. The patches are made from pieces of embroidered, block-printed, painted, resist-dyed and stencilled fabrics (illus 2). Both furnishings and dress cottons, linens and fustians (mixed cotton and linen) are used and a surprisingly large number of Indian fabrics can be identified. Many of these Indian cottons (their import into Britain was forbidden from 1699) are comparable to examples of the earliest known British quilt made in the first decade of the 18th century and now at Levens Hall, Westmoreland, although examples of fashionable European blue resist-dyed cottons included in the Museum's set, suggest 1730 as the likely date of manufacture. This set in particular demonstrates the confident use of the technique in the 18th century and was almost certainly worked professionally.

The largest group of patchwork in the Museum's collection dates from the 19th century and can be divided into two distinctive types; early cotton quilts, and silk furnishings from the second half of the century. This division reflects the development of the craft and changes in the fabrics used for fashionable female dress and interior furnishings. Bed covers from the first quarter of the century show an abundance of beautiful block and plate-printed cottons (*see* pp. 22–46); these illustrate better than any other art form England's greatest period as a centre of cotton printing. A newly acquired marriage quilt given to the Museum by the wife of the descendant of the maker, is as fresh and colourful as the day of completion (p. 30). Not all the cotton quilts in the collection show geometric patterns of this type, however, for a number of examples show *broderie persé* in which flowers and birds are cut out of the print and re-applied to a plain ground. Another superb example shows an enormous variety of shapes of animals and objects cut arbitrarily from patterned fabrics and then pieced together (illus 1). A quite different use of small repeating designed cottons can be seen in a rare pictorial patchwork in which $\frac{1}{4}$in squares are arranged to form a village landscape (illus 4).

Late 19th-century silk patchworks are more formal in pattern and much brighter in colour often using the symmetrical patterns of tumbling blocks and log-cabin designs for cushion covers and other small domestic items. One small table cover of crazy patchwork is lined

*Illus. 4: **Pictorial patchwork hanging** of printed and plain cottons, about 1825.*
(Museum no. T.102–1984)

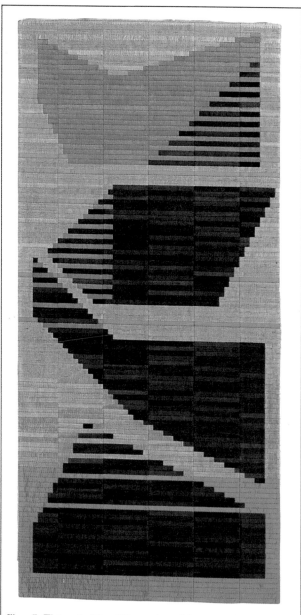

with diagonal stripes of fashionable printed dress silks. It would seem to have been made from samples covering a single year of a manufacturer's production. It is, therefore, an invaluable source for those interested in textiles of the period.

The 20th-century collections include revived traditional techniques including three cushion covers worked by the historian Averil Colby (instructions are provided for two of these) which were acquired by the Museum through the Needlework Development Scheme.

The recent popularity of patchwork has seen the technique widely adopted by crafts people all over the world. Both established and non-traditional patterns are being used and in some cases new technical traditions are being set for future use and adaptation. The Museum's two most recently acquired examples both show very individual and innovatory approaches to the subject. Lucienne Day's hanging 'Flying in Blue' (illus 5), worked in 1985, is an abstract design by one of Britain's most popular and established textile designers. Dinah Prentice, on the other hand, is a painter by training but she has used pieced fabric techniques for over ten years as the most satisfactory vehicle for her own self expression. The Museum has recently acquired a silk panel 'Perspective Drawing' designed and made by her in 1982.

*Illus. 5: **Flying in Blue** Silk patchwork hanging designed and made by Lucienne Day. 1985 (Museum no. T.229–1985)*

LIST OF QUILTS
in the Museum's Collection

(All pieces are English unless otherwise described)

*means a photograph of the quilt is included in this book

18TH-CENTURY PATCHWORK
1475–1902
Coverlet of silks and velvets with hand embroidery; design composed mostly from triangles. Late 18th century.
242toG–1908*
Eight panels for bed hangings. Cotton, linen and fustian in clam shell pattern, c.1730.
T.76–1925
Coverlet of printed cottons with *broderie persé*; design mostly comprising honeycomb hexagons. Late 18th century.
T.37–1934
Fragment of coverlet of painted and printed cottons and linens in hexagon design. Late 18th century.
T.20–1938*
Cot or cushion cover of printed cottons, inscribed 'Henry–Jane Haines September the 17 1786'.
T.102–1938*
Bedcover of printed cottons, multi-patterned design with numbered clock centre which is inscribed 'M C B 1797'.
T.117–1973
Coverlet of silk ribbons. West country, second half of the 18th century.
T.201–1984
Bedcover of silks, braids and velvets with hand embroidery, showing a design which includes squares, rosettes and clam borders, c.1750.

19TH-CENTURY – COTTON PATCHWORK
Circ. 611toM–1920
Dismembered coverlet in squares and triangles. 1820–40.
T.172–1922
Unfinished coverlet of mosaic design. Made by Elizabeth Cakebread, c.1837.
T.17–1924*
Quilt with a ready-printed centre and a design of squares. First half of the 19th century.
T.211–1929
Fragment of quilt of 'Mariner's Compass' design. American, early 19th century.

Circ. 94–1934*
Hanging or quilt of repeating rosette pattern. Third quarter of the 19th century.
T.61–1935
Bedcover of honeycombs and triangles with *broderie persé*. First half of the 19th century.
T.98–1936
Quilt of 'Pineapple' design. American, second half of the 19th century.
T.99–1936*
Quilt of 'Star' design. American, second half of the 19th century.
T.124–1937*
Quilt using a ready-printed centre with design of rectangles and diamonds. Welsh, first half of the 19th century.
T.181–1941
Quilt with ready-printed centre, appliqué decoration and a design of rosettes and triangles. c.1810.
T.1–1944
Quilt with a design of hexagons. Mid-19th century.
T.25–1961
Quilt with a ready-printed centre and design of triangles and lozenges, c.1810.
T.9–1962*
Quilt including appliqué and hand embroidery with figurative centre panel and borders, c.1805.
T.154–1964*
Quilt with 'Mariner's Compass' centre and design of triangles and circles, c.1830.
Circ. 263–1964
Quilt with appliqué details, design mostly worked from triangles, c.1800.
T.196–1965
Coverlet using printed cotton depicting Queen Victoria's Coronation, with border designs of chevrons and diamonds, c.1837.
T.232–1966
Quilt with a design of honeycomb hexagons, 1830–40.

T.59–1967*
Quilt with ready-printed centre and various patterned borders, inscribed 'AEW' and 'IK'. 1830–40.

T.211–1969
Quilt with borders of appliqué, *broderie persé* and patchwork, mostly triangles, c.1820.

T.67–1970
Quilt of patched stripes with appliqué and hand embroidery. Second half of the 19th century.

T.417–1971*
Quilt with design of squares and triangles. Inscribed 'Sarah Wyatt 1801'.

T.128–1972
Coverlet with a design of hexagons and rosettes. 1797–1852.

T.632–1972
Coverlet of zig-zag pattern made from bedhangings worked between 1801 and 1816.

T.340–1977
Quilt with a design of triangles, diamonds, oblongs and squares. English or Welsh. First half of the 19th century.

T.169toTT–1978
Unfinished quilt of honeycomb hexagons with associated pieces. First quarter of the 19th century.

T.154–1979*
Quilt of 'Double Nine-Patch' pattern. Worked by Mrs Whitacre of Montpelier, Indiana. American, late 19th century.

T.2–1982
Quilt with a design of repeating rosettes. First quarter of the 19th century.

T.51–1984
Quilt with appliqué decoration and a design of triangles and squares. c.1805.

T.102–1984*
Pictorial panel of small squares. Second quarter of the 19th century.

T.428–1985*
Wedding quilt of 'Steeple-Jockey' design. Inscribed 'John and Elizabeth Chapman September 19 1829'.

19TH-CENTURY – SILK PATCHWORK
T.241–1932
Man's dressing gown worked in waistcoat silks with a honeycomb design. c.1860–70.

T.75–1937
Quilt of various designs with a feather border. Mid-19th century.

T.76–1937*
Quilt with a design of stars and hexagons. Third quarter of the 19th century.

T.77–1937
Quilt of silks and velvets in design of rosettes, diamonds and hexagons. Third quarter of the 19th century.

T.133–1937
Fire-screen of hexagon pattern. 1870–80.

T.40–1954
Small panel with design of octagons and diamonds. Mid-19th century.

T.110–1954
Panel with design of diamonds. Mid-19th century.

T.118–1959
Coverlet with pattern of hexagons and lozenges. Mid-19th century.

T.178–1966
Unfinished quilt of 'Log cabin' design. c.1870.

T.127–1972
Cover of 'Log cabin' design. Last quarter of the 19th century.

T.266–1979
Cover with a design of rosettes of hexagons. Second half of the 19th century.

T.427–1980*
Unfinished cover of 'Tumbling blocks' design. 1860–70.

T.107–1986
Cover of crazy patchwork with lining of patched stripes. Late 19th century.

19TH-CENTURY – FELTED WOOLLEN PATCHWORK
A.P.27–1917
Picture of pieced, appliqué and hand embroidered felts. 1851.

Circ. 114–1962
Cover showing figurative panels in patchwork and appliqué. c.1856.

20TH-CENTURY PATCHWORK
Circ. 221–1962
Cotton cushion cover (two-sided) called 'Black Frost'. Designed and worked by Averil Colby, 1953.

Circ. 273&A–1962*
Cotton chair seat and back pad. Designed and worked by Averil Colby, 1953.

T.255–1979
Two coloured cotton quilt of 'Star' pattern. Made in Backworth, Northumberland. 1900–1905.

T.229–1985*
Silk hanging 'Flying in Blue'. Designed and worked by Lucienne Day, 1985.

T.2–1987
'Perspective Drawing' silk hanging with painted decoration. Designed and worked by Dinah Prentice, 1982.

TECHNICAL INSTRUCTIONS ON GENERAL QUILT MAKING

In this book, no complicated patchwork techniques are required to make any of the quilts, and even beginners should be able to tackle one of the designs made up of repeated units, such as 'Tumbling Blocks' or 'Grandmother's Garden'; or large simple shapes such as those found in the cot or cushion cover, 'Sarah Wyatt' cotton quilt or the Welsh quilt. Those who like a challenge could try the 'Mariner's Compass', Chequerboard quilt or the Silk quilt.

Most of the quilts are worked in 'pieced' or 'English' patchwork, in which the fabric is cut into geometric shapes and joined to make a bright mosaic of colour, and such quilts are traditionally stitched by hand. One or two of the quilts are made in 'block' patchwork, in which repeating squares made of geometric shapes are stitched together. For these, a sewing machine can be used for all but the smallest pieces, and this will save a great deal of time.

The shapes used in the quilts are hexagons, diamonds, squares, octagons, triangles, segments of circles, trapezoids and rhomboids. Template shapes have been given wherever possible. Some of them are provided at the actual size required to make the quilts, but due to lack of space, others are half-size or even quarter-size, and this is indicated on the relevant pages.

On all templates, there is a $\frac{1}{4}$in seam allowance, but in the cutting guides, on borders and on strips and edges, there is a larger $\frac{1}{2}$in seam allowance. It is difficult to predict precisely the finished size of a quilt, so linings and waddings should be cut to fit once you have completed the piecing of the quilt.

Approximate and generous fabric requirements are given throughout. Cutting guides are arranged so that pieces are cut starting at the centre of the quilt, working outwards.

WHAT YOU NEED FOR PATCHWORK

Fabric   Cotton is the most satisfactory fabric to use for patchwork because it creases sharply and it washes and wears well. Use the same weight of fabric throughout and make sure it is colourfast and pre-shrunk. Do not mix natural and synthetic fibres, because they have different sewing and laundering requirements. Silk can also be used.

Thread   Use fine sewing thread to match the type of fabric you are using. If using more than one colour, work in thread of a neutral shade.

Needles   Stitches should show as little as possible, so sew with fine, sharp needles.

Scissors   A small, sharp pair is best for fine work and a large, sharp pair for cutting out. Keep an old pair for cutting paper templates.

Pins   Use fine, sharp pins. Blunt, thick ones mark the fabric.

Templates   These are the patterns for the shapes, and there are two kinds. Window templates are $\frac{1}{4}$in larger all round than solid templates, to allow for turnings, and they can be laid on the fabric to show how the finished patch will look. Solid templates are the same size as the finished patch and they are the patterns for the papers onto which the patch is sewn. Templates can be bought ready-made of plastic or metal in sets of two, one window and one solid. You can make them quite easily yourself out of thick card, though. If you are doing this, draw them first on graph paper if possible, and then stick them to card. Don't forget that accuracy is all-important.

Other useful items   Thimble, lead pencil, thin card (such as greetings cards), graph paper, a cutting board, isometric paper (for drawing hexagons), and a tape measure.

PREPARING PATCHWORK SHAPES

The easiest shapes to sew are the ones with wide angles, such as hexagons and octagons. To sew a patch round a wide-angled paper template:

1 Pin the paper template to the centre of the wrong side of the patch, with two sides on the straight grain of the fabric. Fold the seam allowance of one of the straight edges over the paper, then fold the other edges tight up against the paper.

2 Make a knot in the thread and tack through the folded edge of the fabric and paper, starting about a third of the way along.

3 Fold the fabric over the next edge and tack through the fold at the corner, bringing up the stitch about a third of the way along this side. Continue like this all round the patch, tacking down each corner.

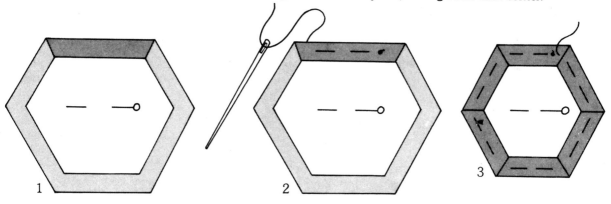

Diamonds and other pointed shapes

Triangles, trapezoids and rhomboids are slightly more difficult to sew because of the points, which have to be folded down.

1 Pin the paper template to the centre of the wrong side of the patch, with two sides on the straight grain of the fabric. Working towards the point, fold the seam allowance of one edge of the shape tightly against the template.

2 Make a knot in the thread and tack along this folded edge through fabric and paper. When you reach the point, fold down the second edge so that it lies parallel to the edge of the paper. Do not stitch down.

3 Fold the second edge over the paper so that it encloses the previous fold and tack through the fold at the corner. At the next corner make a fold as for the hexagon and at the next sharp point repeat the double fold. Tack to the fourth point and finish as for the hexagon.

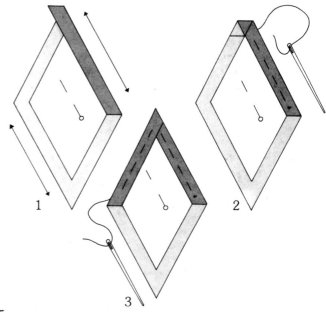

SEWING THE PATCHES TOGETHER

Oversew the patches together on the wrong side. Try not to catch the papers when sewing, as this makes it difficult to remove them when the work is finished. Remove the paper templates at the last minute, before lining.

When sewing patches without paper templates, the sewing line must be marked on the wrong side of the fabric, on the inside edge of the window template, in pencil.

When sewing by machine, use window templates to make the patches (as described above) and pin the patches together at the joins with pins placed perpendicular to the line being sewn. You can machine over the pins, which saves tacking time.

ASSEMBLING

It is important to assemble patches and squares in the right order, so plan well in advance. When possible, join small pieces together so that they form bigger strips, squares or borders. Join triangles so that they form squares or strips. Do not join straight fabric to bias fabric unless the design calls for it. Make sure all seams meet exactly. Press seams towards the darkest fabric, and not open.

QUILTING

Patchwork often looks even better when it is quilted, for the two crafts complement each other

Quilting is the fastening of two layers of fabric with a layer of wadding in between, using either knots or stitches. On a patchwork quilt, the quilting can follow the outline of a shape or it can follow a seam or it can form a pattern or series of patterns of its own. Quilting can be done by hand or machine.

WHAT YOU NEED FOR QUILTING

Fabric   Cotton, silk, fine wool and fine linen are all suitable for quilting. Use a matching fabric for lining.
Wadding   Cotton wadding may be used and it is even possible to use old blankets. The easiest, and most practical and lightweight, however, is the synthetic wadding obtainable from many department stores.
Templates   You can make templates by tracing a design on to cardboard and cutting it out.

Pins and needles   These must be fine and sharp, to avoid making holes.
Other useful items   Scissors, quilting thread, thimble, chalk pencil, lead pencil, lightweight cardboard, ruler, craft knife, and dressmaker's carbon paper.

PREPARING FOR QUILTING

1   Iron the top layer of fabric and mark out the quilting pattern on the right side in chalk pencil, lead pencil or dressmaker's carbon paper.
2   Iron the lining and smooth the wadding.
3   Lay the lining flat on a table right side downwards and pat it smooth.
4   Lay the wadding on top of this and pat it smooth.
5   Place the top fabric, right side up, on top of the wadding.
6   Pin the three layers together, starting from the middle and working outwards.
7   Tack the three layers together from the centre outwards. Tacks should be not more than two inches apart. Leave all tacking stitches in until the quilting is completed.

Quilting can be done on a quilting frame, in small sections on an embroidery hoop, or be held in the hand. It is usually done on a frame so that one hand is above and the other is below the frame to guide the point of the needle.

Hand quilting

Using a single strand of thread and short lengths, start sewing in the centre of the work and quilt outwards with small, evenly-spaced running stitches. There should be about five to seven stitches to the inch and it is important that the stitches are even.

Machine quilting

Work must be well tacked for machine quilting. Hold the work flat with your hands on either side of the machine foot, so that the seam is visible.

FINISHING OFF A QUILT

1 Binding with the top.

If the top is large enough, it can be turned over to the back to make a neat edge. Trim the top, wadding and lining all round, turn in the raw edges and fold the top edge over the back. Pin, tack and hem in place.

2 Strip binding.

Join strips of bias fabric with diagonal seams, as shown in the diagrams. Sew the strip to the top of the quilt, then turn the strip over to the back and sew it in place.

3 Quilting edge.

Trim the edges of the lining and the top and turn them in. Trim the wadding close to the sewing line. Tack, and then join the top and lining with two rows of running stitches.

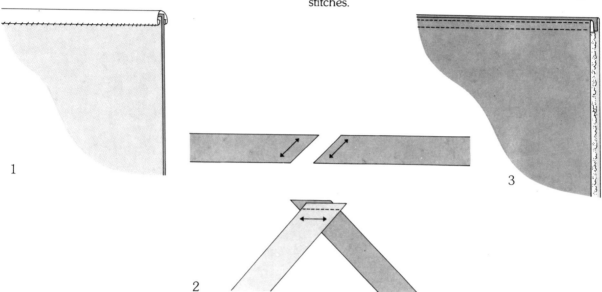

MEASUREMENTS

The measurements in this book are all given as imperial. For those who prefer to work in metric the following chart will help conversions. However, it should be remembered that metric measurements will never be the exact conversion of imperial and the resulting quilt may alter slightly in proportions.

CONVERSION CHART

Inches	$\frac{1}{32}$	$\frac{1}{16}$	$\frac{1}{8}$	$\frac{1}{4}$	$\frac{1}{2}$	$\frac{3}{4}$	1	2	3	4
Millimetres	0·8	1·6	3	6	12·5	10	25	50	76	101

Inches	5	6	7	8	9	10	11	12	24	36
Millimetres	127	152	177	203	228	254	279	304	609	914

COT OR CUSHION COVER

Embroidered cotton patchwork cot or cushion cover
English: 1786
Length 22in × 23in

This quilt is one of seven examples of 18th-century patchwork in the Museum collection. This modest panel has a simple but effective design of a patchwork border with a framed centre of windmill triangles. Only six different, but highly fashionable, patterned cottons have been used and the panel shows no evidence of either interlining or quilting.

The central panel is embroidered with black wool in chain stitch, a technique which became particularly popular following the import of Indian embroideries into Europe from the 17th century. The inscription is embroidered in cross stitch in much the same manner as contemporary children's samplers. The two crowns, similarly worked, were also popular sampler motifs, forming part of a young girl's training in the correct marking of linen of large households. This would form part of her duties if she went into service.

No information concerning the history of this patchwork was available when it was acquired in 1938, but the inscription, announcing the birth of a child to Henry and Jane Haines on 17th September 1786, suggest that the panel was prepared as a christening present for the baby.

Given by Miss G. M. Major   (Museum no. T.20–1938)

INSTRUCTIONS

This interesting old cushion cover in creams, browns and subdued prints is enlivened by delicate black embroidery in chain stitch.

There is a central 6in square of four dark and four light-coloured triangles, which is surrounded by 1in and 1½in wide strips of patterned fabrics. Surrounding this are the 3½in wide embroidered strips and the final strip is composed of 2¼in squares made of light and dark coloured triangles.

Quantities are given in terms of light and dark tones. ½in seam allowances are provided on the strips. The cushion cover is unquilted.

Materials

9in × 36in dark-toned patterned fabric
12in × 36in plain cream fabric
18in × 36in various patterned light fabrics
Lining to fit

Cutting guide

4 dark coloured triangles (template 1)
4 light coloured triangles (template 1)
2 patterned strips 9in × 2in
2 patterned strips 7in × 2in
2 patterned strips 12in × 2½in
2 patterned strips 9in × 2½in
2 plain cream strips 19in × 4½in
2 plain cream strips 12in × 4½in
36 dark coloured triangles (template 2)
36 light coloured triangles (template 2)

To make

Piece all the large triangles together to make squares and join two squares to make a strip. Join the two strips to make a larger square.

Piece the small triangles to make squares, then join them to make strips of ten and eight squares. Join the narrow borders to the central squares. Then join on the cream border and finally the outer border.
Embroider the cream strip.

This cushion cover could be made by machine and then hand embroidered.

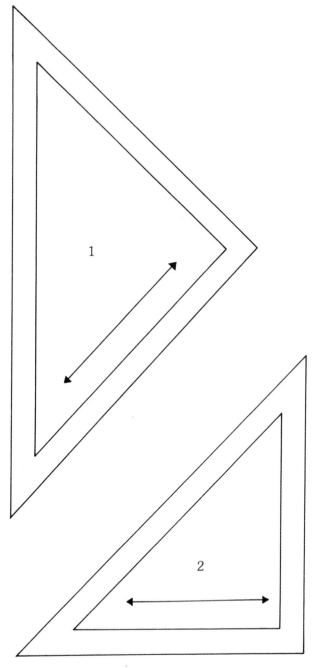

1

2

Section of embroidery.

COTTON QUILT
'Sarah Wyatt, 1801'

Cotton patchwork quilt
English: 1801
Length 86in × 83in

This patchwork quilt has a framed central design with a border of triangles giving the effect of diamonds or windmills, depending on the distribution of light and dark patterned cottons. The central panel is formed from four windmill squares and shows the same sequence of cottons throughout, the two lower squares being a mirror image of the upper two. Despite the maker having adapted the cottons to fit, the misalignment of squares at one end of the quilt is deliberate and follows an early pattern tradition of shaping the top to fit around pillows at the head of the bed.

The quilt is interlined with wool and lined with white cotton. The elaborate overall quilting is worked in white cotton and is very similar to work found on plain embroidered and quilted covers of the 18th century. The quilting pattern shows a central square surrounded by four borders of zig-zag lines and circles filled with flowerheads and diaper patterns. Hearts also figure prominently in the quilting pattern and may indicate that the quilt was prepared for an engagement, marriage, birth or as a gift to a young girl.

There are 21 different, small repeating, printed cottons used in the patchwork showing a predominance of madder printed pink patterns. The oldest cotton used is a floral trail design which can be dated to the 1770s and the border is a design of oak leaves in pink and brown on a figured ground. On the cotton backing of the quilt is embroidered 'Sarah + Wyatt 1801' worked in blue silk in cross stitch. The quilt was embroidered by the great grandmother of the donor.

Given by Miss R. E. Chick   (Museum no. T.417–1971)

23

INSTRUCTIONS

In this quilt, large triangles have been arranged to form a pattern of large squares, but, as in many old quilts, the maker clearly made up the pattern as she went along and it does not quite fit together symmetrically. She had to cheat a little here and there, adding strips to make some squares wider.

The quilt is worked in eight different shades and patterns of pink, and some blue, which make up 16in squares. The placing of the light and dark triangles is random, an effect which can easily be copied in modern fabrics. However, for those who prefer more precision, the plan showing the placing of dark tones can be followed, leaving the choice of medium and light tones to the maker. The resulting quilt should be square. To make the quilt fit a bed, then, a wider border should be added top and bottom, say 10in each end and a narrower one of, say, 5in at the sides. This will make a quilt measuring 100in × 90in. The quilt is quilted all over.

Materials

$1\frac{1}{2}$yd × 36in pink patterned fabric (for strips)
3yd × 36in pink patterned fabric (for borders)
3yd × 36in dark pink patterned fabric (dark triangles)
3yd × 36in various patterned pink fabrics (for paler triangles)
$\frac{3}{4}$yd × 36in blue fabric
Wadding and lining to fit

Cutting guide

84 triangles in various pink and blue patterned fabrics (template 1)
84 triangles in dark pink patterned fabric (template 1)
4 strips 33in × 9in patterned strip fabric
2 borders 101in × 11in in border fabric
2 borders 91in × 6in in border fabric

To make

Sew the triangles together in pairs of light and dark to make squares. Assemble 16 of these squares to form the central square and add the 33in strips to each side with a pieced square at each corner. The remaining two-colour squares make up the rest of the pattern.

Add the narrow side borders and the wider end borders.

Tack wadding and lining to the finished top, and quilt. This quilt could be made by machine.

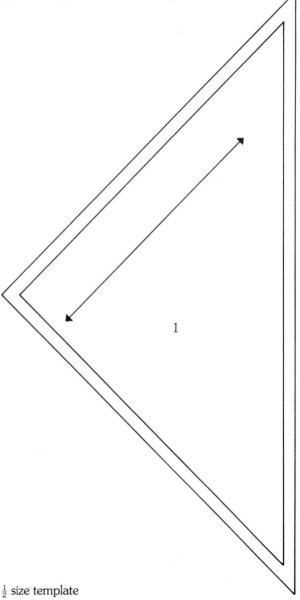

1

$\frac{1}{2}$ size template

24

25

BEDCOVER
'King George Reviewing the Troops'

Detail of a cotton patchwork bedcover
English: about 1805
Length approx. 111in × 111in
Detail shown: approx. 9in × 12in
For complete quilt see Illus. 3

Because of the complicated composition of this bedcover just two details of the repeating background are included.

This patchwork bedcover is made of plain and printed cottons with additional embroidery in the central panel and border worked with coloured silks in chain, satin and long and short stitches.

The ground pattern has a repeating design of segmented circles of different patterns and variations. The centre shows a circular pictorial panel possibly representing one of two reviews of volunteers by George III which took place on 26th and 28th October 1803. Above this panel are representations of the sun and moon which appear below again in segments of a circle. There is a broad border outlined by triangles which shows domestic scenes and incidents of military and naval life. It is probable that these vignettes were copied from contemporary prints which provided embroiderers with a major source for pictorial designs at this time.

The Mariner's Compass design used in the patchwork emphasizes the naval theme of the bedcover which was worked at a period of intense national euphoria following England's naval successes against the French and Spanish fleets. A number of printed cottons manufactured at this time also show naval themes, especially Nelson's victories and his death at Trafalgar in October 1805.

Given by Mrs Gertrude S. Farraby   (Museum no. T.9–1962)

INSTRUCTIONS

Surrounding the central panel depicting King George reviewing his troops are the small Mariner's Compasses together with other patterns in circles, each one $5\frac{1}{2}$in in diameter. The designs of the circles vary slightly, but the colours, in very subdued prints, are much the same in each. Instructions for making only two of these circles are provided.

The first is an eight-point mariner's compass with a central $1\frac{3}{4}$in cross sewn onto a $1\frac{3}{4}$in diameter circle. This arrangement is, in turn, sewn on to a circle $2\frac{1}{2}$in in diameter. The outer circle is composed of pieced shapes, which are given in the templates.

The second circle is more complicated, composed of a great many little segments which fit together to form the circle. $\frac{1}{4}$in seam allowances are given on the circles.

Materials
Scraps of cotton fabric in suitable colours

Cutting guide for Circle 1
1 circle $2\frac{1}{4}$in diameter
Cross shape (template 1)
1 circle 3in diameter
1 circle $3\frac{3}{4}$in diameter
8 shapes (template 2)
8 shapes (template 3)

Cutting guide for Circle 2
1 shape (template 1)
8 shapes (template 2)
8 shapes (template 3)
12 shapes (template 4)
12 shapes (template 5)
12 shapes (template 6)

To make Circle 1
Appliqué the cross to the circle, and appliqué this circle to the two successive circles. Piece the outer circle, using paper templates as described in the introduction. Sew to the completed inner circle. Remove papers.

To make Circle 2
Using paper templates, piece the circles together, making the compass first, then the outer circle. Remove papers.

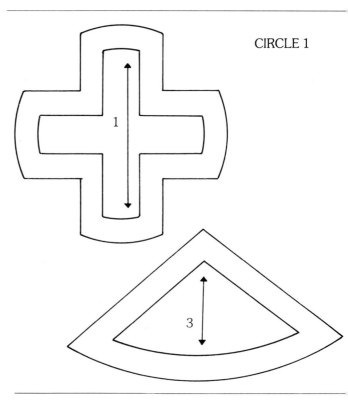

CIRCLE 1

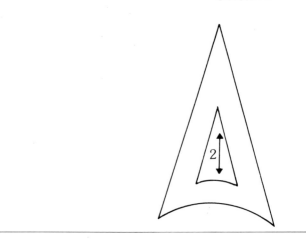

CIRCLE 2

28

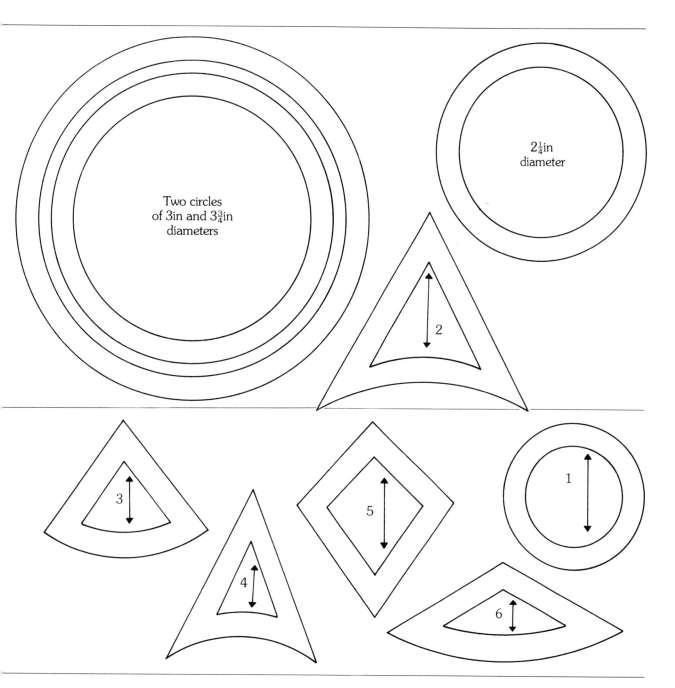

Two circles
of 3in and $3\frac{3}{4}$in
diameters

$2\frac{1}{4}$in
diameter

WEDDING QUILT

Cotton patchwork wedding quilt
English: 1829
Length 106in × 98in
Border width 14½in

A bedcover of repeating 'steeplechase' or 'jockey' patchwork surrounding a 12in square block-printed quilt centre commemorating the Duke of Wellington's victory at the Battle of Vittoria in 1813. Under the central floral panel, a rectangle of plain white linen is inscribed with a charming verse reminding the husband of many of his wife's good qualities, worked with blue silk in cross stitch. Also embroidered are the names 'John and Elizabeth Chapman. September 19 1829'.

The patchwork utilizes a great variety of block-printed cottons of various designs and colours all dating from the first quarter of the 19th century. The quilt's wide border (not shown) is a roller-printed cotton of floral design of the 1890s, a much later addition. The fact that the printed quilt centre was not used for 16 years after the event commemorated, shows how sought after and cherished these accessories were.

Said to have been prepared for the Chapman wedding, the patchwork was never finished. It is unlined and the tacking threads are still in place. Printed and hand-written papers are still visible at the back of the quilt and, despite family tradition believing these to be love letters, they were cut from advertisements, children's writing exercises and pages from household accounts.

Given by Mrs Gwendolyn Baker in memory of her husband Stephen Baker, great nephew of the quilt's maker Elizabeth Chapman.   (Museum no. T.428–1985)

INSTRUCTIONS

The design, which is in muted colours, depends on the arrangement of the dark and light tones of each set of four squares. There are 15 sets of four squares across the quilt and 17 sets on each side. Each small square contains a quarter of a segment of a circle in a contrasting tone, the quarters of the four squares fitting together to form a complete circle. Each complete circle has two light-and two dark-toned quarter circles in a contrasting light or dark-toned square. The darks and lights face each other diagonally.

Each small square measures $2\frac{1}{4}$in square and the quilt, with its $14\frac{1}{2}$in border, needs 255 sets of squares without a central panel, or 246 with.

Materials

2yd × 36in dark-toned, patterned fabric
2yd × 36in light-toned, patterned fabric
3yd × 36in border fabric
12in × 12in square of floral fabric
Lining to fit

Cutting guide (without panel)

510 of shape A in dark fabric (template 1)
510 of shape B in dark fabric (template 2)
510 of shape A in light fabric (template 1)
510 of shape B in light fabric (template 2)
2 strips measuring $68\frac{1}{2}$in × $15\frac{1}{2}$in, for top and bottom
2 strips measuring $106\frac{1}{2}$in × $15\frac{1}{2}$in, for side borders

To make

Sew the dark B shapes to the light A shapes and the light B shapes to the dark A shapes.

When sewing curves, run a line of stitching inside the seam line of the inward curve and clip into the seam allowance with sharp scissors up to, but not into, the seam line. Pin, tack and sew the inner curve to fit the outer curve.

Sew the completed squares in straight strips, with all seams matching, then sew the strips together. Sew on the borders. These will look better if the corners are mitred, in which case the end borders must be cut $96\frac{1}{2}$in long.

Remove papers and press, pressing curved seams toward the inward curves.

Sew the patchwork to the lining, catching the top at intervals to prevent the quilt ballooning.

Some of this quilt could be pieced by machine.

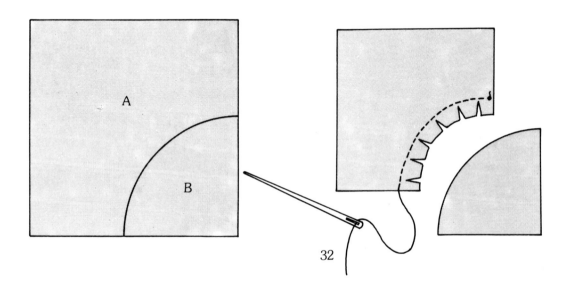

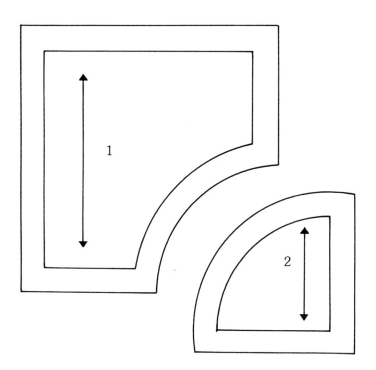

FRAMED 'MARINER'S COMPASS'

Cotton patchwork quilt
English: about 1830
Length 101½in × 96in

Patchwork bedcover showing a framed central triple star, or 'Mariner's Compass', design with borders of various geometric patterns including long triangles, segmented squares and repeating box patterns of rhomboids.

The fashion for densely patterned and coloured textiles which developed in the second quarter of the 19th century is shown to perfection in this patchwork. Many of the cottons used date from the mid-1820s. They were originally glazed but despite the use of a great variety of colourful geometric, floral and paisley cone patterns the overall effect is of a blurred sepia brown colouring. The outer border, in particular, gives the effect of tortoiseshell or walnut burr, both popular decorative finishes of the period.

The quilt is lined with white cotton and interlined with a thick matted wool. Although it is not visible on the top of the bedcover, the ground is quilted with work of a very high standard, showing a central star with geometric borders which roughly correspond in design to the patchwork except for one wide quilted outer border which shows the running feather design popular with North Country quilters.

Given by Miss A. M. Johns   (Museum no. T.154–1964)

35

INSTRUCTIONS

The original quilt was totally pieced whereas the instructions here include some appliqué work. Also, only the central 52in square has instructions provided. Set within a 20in square, the diameter of the circle of the 16-point 'Mariner's Compass' is 18in. Four points of the compass predominate, so there is no central circle from which the points radiate. The compass points are in two tones of fabric.

The compass circle is sewn to a quilted square which has a red square at each corner. Around the central square are three borders, two are 4in wide, and one is 8in wide. They are made up of square diamonds, rhomboids and triangles. Beyond this is a design of 'steeplechase' squares, instructions for which are given on page 32.

As colours used will depend on personal preference and availability of fabrics, quantities are given in terms of light and dark and red. The rhomboids in the outer band could be made in alternating light and dark tones, which would give an interesting three-dimensional effect and complement that of the compass.

In the original there are irregularities in the placing of the triangles. These have been corrected in the chart.

Materials

3yd × 36in dark fabric
1½yd × 36in light fabric
18in × 36in red fabric
Wadding and lining to fit

Cutting guide for Compass

4 red, 4 light shapes (template 1)
4 light, 4 dark shapes (template 3)
8 light, 8 dark shapes (template 2)
19in circle of light fabric
21in square of light fabric
4 red squares (template 7)

Cutting guide for Border A

24 patterned squares (template 4)
44 triangles (template 5)
8 half triangles (template 5A)

Cutting guide for Border B

28 light, 24 dark triangles (template 6)
8 dark half triangles (template 6A)

4 light, 4 dark triangles (template 8)

Cutting guide for Border C

44 squares (template 4)
84 light, 92 dark rhomboids (template 9)
40 light, 40 dark triangles (template 5)
8 light, 8 dark half triangles (template 5A)

To make

Piece the compass shapes to make a star 18in across. Appliqué the finished star to the circle and then to centre of the 21in square. Appliqué red squares in each corner.

Make up the strips in order in the photograph, noting the placing of the light and dark tones. Join the outer strips to the centre square, as in the photograph. Line and quilt.

Much of the piecing of the outer borders could be done by machine.

All templates are ½ size

WELSH QUILT

Cotton patchwork quilt
Welsh: first half of the 19th century
Length 94in × 83in

This is the only patchwork in the Museum collection with a known Welsh provenance. The donor lived in Pwllheli, Carnarvonshire when the quilt was given to the Museum, but it is not known if this is where it was made.

The framed octagonal design is very simple in construction and all the component pieces are large. Unity is provided, however, by very beautiful quilting which is particularly evident in the outer borders. Large patchwork compositions have always been favoured by Welsh quiltmakers as this makes the quilting easier to sew and the patterns are shown to better advantage. In this example, the clever framing of the central octagon with a strip of plain white cotton has provided an opportunity to produce one of the simplest but most effective quilting patterns, a repeating twist. It would not be noticeable if worked on a patterned ground.

The composition of the quilt is likely to have been developed during construction rather than been designed in advance. Despite this, the patchwork is symmetrical in colour and pattern, except for a wide pillow border set in at the top end of the quilt.

Most of the cottons used were originally glazed. The central section shows two large-scale printed designs both dating from 1815 to 1820 whereas the most recent cotton, a repeating rosebud pattern on a black ground, dates from the 1840s. The quilt is lined with a finely woven cotton and interlined with cotton wool.

Given by Miss Margaret Evans   (Museum no. T.124–1937)

INSTRUCTIONS

This richly-quilted bed cover is slightly irregular in design, for, as can be seen in the photograph, the corner blocks are all different sizes. However, the quilt still ends up as a rectangle and is none the worse for its uneven patches.

The central square, set on its corner and trimmed to an octagon with white triangles, measures 19in. This is surrounded by a quilted border and a further floral border with $2\frac{1}{2}$in dark-coloured squares at each corner and two more borders composed of squares and triangles at one end to lengthen it.

The quilt is finished by a plain strip border richly decorated with quilting stitches. To create the same effect in modern fabrics, the bed cover would have to be quilted with many different patterns for which one pattern is provided. The arrangement of colours would also have to be followed closely.

Materials

$1\frac{1}{2}$yd × 36in black patterned fabric
$1\frac{1}{2}$yd × 36in floral patterned fabric
3yd × 36in varied patterned fabrics
$2\frac{1}{2}$yd × 36in border fabric
Wadding and lining to fit

Cutting guide

Note: $\frac{1}{2}$in seam allowance given except on templates
18in square of floral fabric
4 white triangles (template 1)
4 white strips, 25in × $3\frac{1}{2}$in
4 $3\frac{1}{2}$in squares in blue fabric
4 triangles 25in base and 17in sides in floral fabric
2 strips 33in × 5in, floral fabric
2 strips 33in × 5in, striped fabric
4 squares in black spotted fabric (template 2)
24 triangles (template 3)
6 8in squares (top and bottom)
20 triangles (template 4)
8 $6\frac{3}{4}$in squares (sides)
4 rectangles 9in × 11in
4 rectangles 5in × 11in
4 rectangles 13in × 6in
14 triangles (template 5)
4 triangles (template 6)
7 triangles (template 7)
2 triangles (template 8)
2 border strips 9in × 81in
2 border strips 9in × 95in

To make

Cut the central square on the straight of the fabric and sew on triangles at the corners. Sew on the white strips next, and cover the ends of the strips with small blue squares.

Turn the square diagonally and piece the quilt in the order shown, joining first the triangles in strips, then the squares set diagonally in strips, then all these strips together. Quilt when piecing is complete.

This quilt could be made by machine.

A quilting example

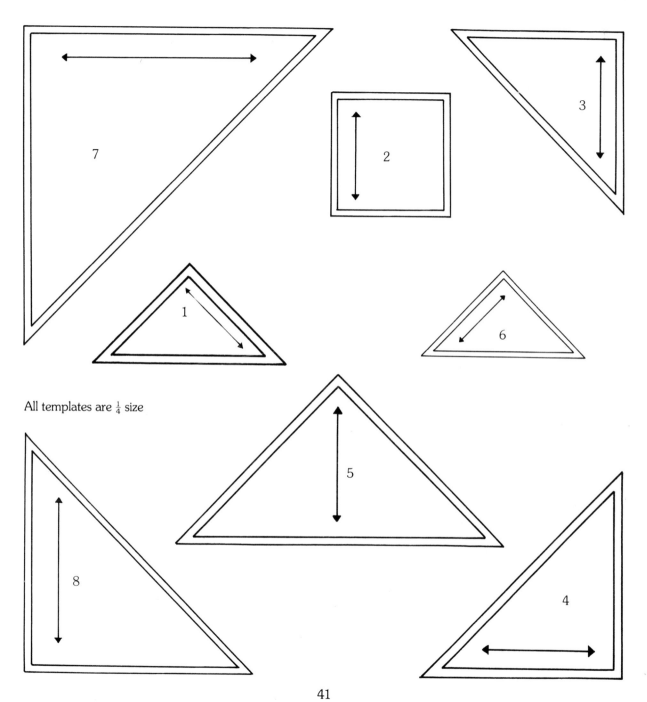

All templates are $\frac{1}{4}$ size

COTTON QUILT WITH BORDERS

Cotton patchwork quilt
English: 1830–40
Length 113in × 122in

The most varied patchwork composition in the collection, this quilt is also the most intricately designed; each border being symmetrical in colour and pattern.

The centre shows an unusually large block-printed panel ($23\frac{1}{2} \times 25\frac{1}{2}$in) dating from the late 1820s. The border designs show dog's tooth triangles, linked squares, zig-zag triangles, rosettes of hexagons and pyramid triangles with occasional plain borders of vertically striped fabric. Each of the patterned stripes has a corner design and, as well as using ready-printed panels, the maker has cut stars, rosettes, and flowers and applied them to a white ground.

Apart from the central panel, dress cottons are used exclusively in this quilt and examples of dark blue, resist dyed patterns date from the beginning of the 19th century. The rest of the cottons date from 1825 and the quilt can be dated by the latest examples which include a brown print of the 1830s seen in the outer border.

The initials 'AEW' and 'IK' are embroidered with blue silk in cross stitch on the central printed panel and the whole is lined with white linen and quilted with an overall zig-zag pattern in cotton thread.

It is appropriate that such an interesting quilt (which was bought from the Ladies Work Society) was donated in memory of the late Peter Floud, who, while on the staff of the Museum, pioneered work on the history of English printed cottons.

Given by Jason W. Westerfield   (Museum no. T.59–1967)

INSTRUCTIONS

Instructions are only provided for the border designs of this large quilt which demonstrate just how effective a broad border can be. Made up of bands of various patterns, the width of the finished border is about 32in. The fabric requirements given here are for a 36in length of border and $\frac{1}{4}$in seams are allowed for.

The border surrounds a central square of floral fabric which is framed by a strip of striped fabric and the whole bed cover is quilted diagonally.

Colours used will depend on choice and availability and have been described here as coloured (i.e. variegated colours), white or patterned. The bands are made up as follows:

Band 1: A $5\frac{3}{4}$in strip made up of coloured squares set on their corners to make a pair of diamonds. These are contrasted with white squares and triangles.

Band 2: A $4\frac{1}{2}$in strip of coloured right-angled triangles separated from each other by white strips.

Band 3: A 5in strip of 1in hexagon rosettes set on a background of white hexagons.

Band 4: A $6\frac{1}{2}$in strip of coloured, striped fabric.

Band 5: A $6\frac{1}{4}$in strip of large triangles placed one on top of the other, interspersed with white triangles.

Band 6: A 4in strip of patterned fabric.

The shapes in bands 1, 3 and 5 could all be appliquéd to a plain white background.

Band 1

Materials
Scraps of different coloured fabrics
12in × 36in white fabric
Cutting guide
24 squares in different coloured fabrics (template 1)
26 half squares in white fabric (template 1a)
11 squares in white fabric (template 1)
To make
Sew the squares and triangles together in strips of five, alternating the colours as in the photograph. Join these strips together to form a band $6\frac{1}{4}$in wide, placing the squares so that they touch point to point.

Band 2

Materials
6in × 36in coloured fabrics

$2\frac{1}{2}$in × 36in white fabric
Cutting guide
9 complete and 2 half triangles in coloured fabric (templates 2 and 2A)
$1\frac{1}{4}$in wide strips in white fabric, cut on the straight.
To make
Sew the coloured triangles to the white strips in the order shown on the photograph and in the diagram to make one long strip 5in wide.

Band 3

Materials
8in × 36in different patterned fabrics
10in × 36in white fabric
Cutting guide
42 shapes in different coloured fabrics (template 3)
61 shapes in white fabric (template 3)
To make
Sew the hexagons together to make 6 rosettes, each one measuring $5\frac{1}{2}$in. Sew white hexagons between and at the sides of each rosette.

Band 4

Materials and cutting guide
Cut a band of striped fabric 7in × 36in

Band 5

Materials
8in × 36in coloured fabrics
8in × 36in white fabric
Cutting guide
12 large triangles in coloured fabrics (template 4)
24 small triangles in white fabric (template 5)
To make
Sew two white and one coloured triangle together, then join these sections to form a strip measuring $6\frac{3}{4}$in.

Band 6

Materials and cutting guide
Cut a strip of patterned fabric $4\frac{1}{2}$in × 36in

Join all the completed strips. Cut wadding and lining to fit and quilt. All these bands, except that composed of hexagons, could be made by machine.

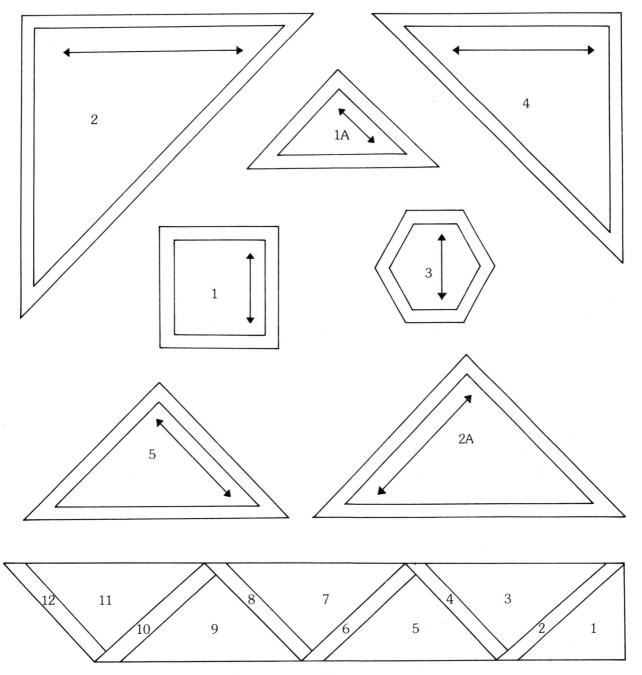

CHEQUERBOARD QUILT

Cotton patchwork quilt
English: first half of the 19th century
Length 107in × 104½in

This is another example of a quilt using a ready-printed centre, this time a bouquet of flowers. There are five such quilts in the Museum collection, three are described in this book, two others show baskets of flowers with a commemorative inscription celebrating George III's Golden Jubilee. In this patchwork, the octagon centre has a separate printed border but the designs of both are rather overshadowed by the block of over 200 tiny patchwork squares which surrounds them.

A great variety of printed cottons are used and these include dress patterns and men's shirtings of brushed cotton. Designs show Turkey-red 'paisley' cones and other Indian inspired patterns, small floral designs, shaded stripes, checks and spotted fabrics. One large square, in the top left hand corner, was cut from a printer's end; the remnant at the end of a roll of printed cotton which is usually discarded. It is interesting to speculate whether the maker obtained such scraps from the factory direct or from her local draper.

The quilt is interlined with a coarse, hand-woven woollen fabric and quilted through the two top layers in a design of repeating 6in squares. The lining of a brown printed cotton was applied after quilting and is attached with random single stitches.

Given by Mrs Marchant   (Museum no. T.17–1924)

INSTRUCTIONS

The central, irregular panel depicting a bouquet of flowers is set in a square composed of over 200 $\frac{1}{2}$in squares. This, in turn, is surrounded by an octagonal border squared off by dark-coloured triangles. The central square is set diamond-fashion within a 16 square border, dark squares alternating with light. The light squares are themselves a chequerboard design of 81 $\frac{1}{2}$in squares set in a $\frac{3}{4}$in border.

Around this is another border. Blocks of 16 $1\frac{1}{2}$in squares alternate with more blocks of the tiny $\frac{1}{2}$in squares and round this is a border of patterned fabric blocks and tiny squares. So, although the design of the quilt looks somewhat complicated, the patchwork is, in fact, composed only of squares of three different sizes: a plain 6in square; a 6in square divided into 16 $1\frac{1}{2}$in squares of alternating light and dark colours; and a bordered 6in square containing 81 $\frac{1}{2}$in squares. The overall composition of the quilt concentrates on the symmetrical arrangement of these three units and the balancing of pattern and tone with strong colours blending together subtly to give soft shades.

The actual colours used will depend on the choice and availability of fabric so they have been described in terms of light and dark tones. Quantities of fabric and measurements are provided only for the central 54in square and $\frac{1}{4}$in turnings are given on all measurements. There is some quilting.

Materials

12in × 12in of floral fabric
2yd × 36in of light-coloured, different patterned fabrics
2yd × 36in of dark-coloured, different patterned fabrics
Lining and wadding to fit

Cutting guide

1 slightly elongated octagon shape $11\frac{1}{2}$in × $8\frac{1}{2}$in
4 dark triangles (template 1)
4 strips $12\frac{1}{2}$ × $3\frac{1}{2}$in floral pattern fabric
28 $6\frac{1}{2}$in squares in patterned fabrics
64 2in squares in dark patterned fabric
64 2in squares in light patterned fabric
Approx. 1500 1in squares in dark patterned fabric
Approx. 1500 1in squares in light patterned fabric
$1\frac{1}{2}$in strips in dark or light fabric for edging small squares

To make

Piece the central panel, stitching the tiny squares to form a square around the octagon. All the squares made up of $\frac{1}{2}$in squares also have a $\frac{3}{4}$in border of floral strips. Add dark triangles at the corners to form a square.

Join the squares in strips in the sequence shown in the photograph. The piecing of the small squares should be done by hand but the larger ones could be sewn by machine.

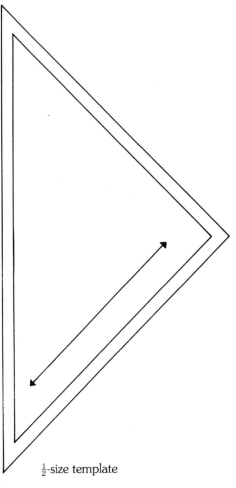

$\frac{1}{2}$-size template

48

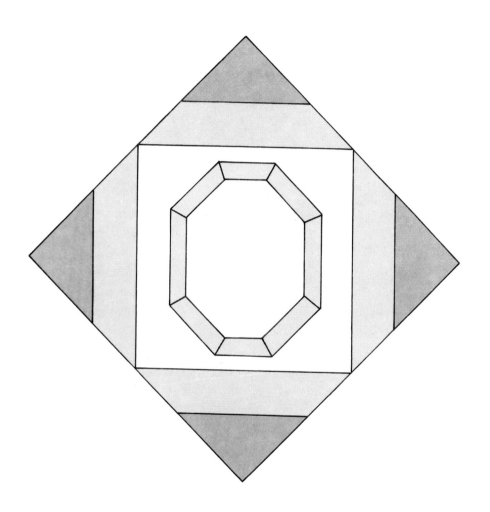

'TUMBLING BLOCKS'

Unfinished silk patchwork
English: 1860s–70s
Length 70in × 55in

This unfinished panel of patchwork is worked in the 'Tumbling Blocks' design in which units of three equally-sized diamond blocks fit together to give a *trompe l'oeil* effect of three-dimensional boxes seen from above. Because the sides of the panel incorporate half-blocks, it is probable that these were the intended finished edges. The panel, therefore, was possibly made as a curtain or as a cover for a single bed.

A noticeable change in the materials and patterns of patchwork can be seen from the middle of the 19th century. Following the changing fashions of female dress, silk again became popular for quiltmaking and repeating designs replaced more complex compositions. Colour rather than shape became the most important factor and with the discovery of aniline dyestuffs from 1856 (when 'Perkin's mauve' was first seen), the effects of these bright colours on woven silks provided the maker with an endless variety of colour and texture.

Plain and patterned jacquard-woven dress and waistcoat silks and ribbons are used in the quilt and these show a number of popular technical effects including *chiné*, ribbon stripes, tartans and brocading. One silk uses a woven pictorial design of fashionable ladies' headgear, showing a silk bonnet and a straw hat of the early 1860s.

The patchwork is unlined and the outer edge still has paper patterns sewn into the back with tacking stitches. These show the technique and direction used by the maker; the papers and tackings being removed as each new line of pattern was attached.

Given by Mr W. R. Hall   (Museum no. T.427–1980)

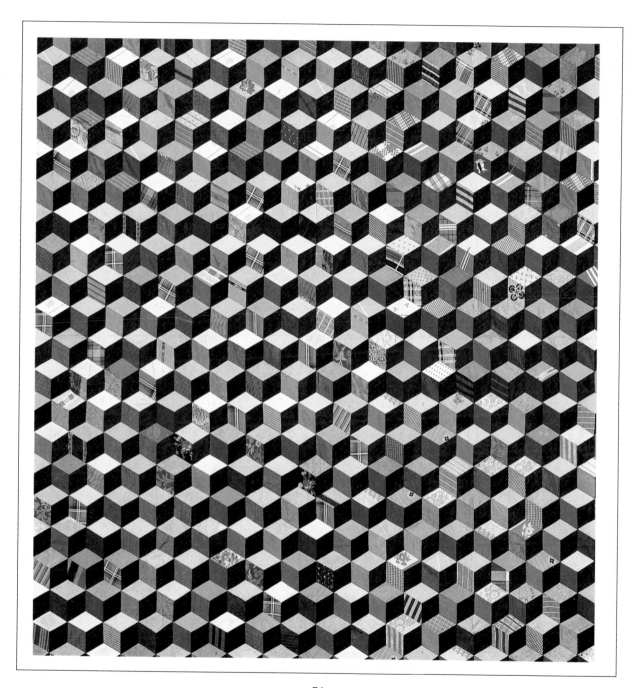

51

INSTRUCTIONS

The 'Tumbling Block' (or 'Baby Block') design has always been popular with patchworkers. It is made entirely of diamonds in three tones – light, medium, and dark. These are put together in an ordered sequence to resemble the three-dimensional cubes which give this type of design its name. The diamonds here are short, with $1\frac{3}{4}$in sides.

Colours chosen will depend on choice and availability, so quantities are described in terms of tones. The dark tones here are all black, giving a dramatic effect against the brightly-coloured, medium and light-toned silks, though any other very dark colour would give the same three-dimensional effect.

The quilt could be copied in silks, though patchwork is more durable in cottons. This silk version is unquilted.

Materials
3yd × 36in dark-toned fabric
3yd × 36in medium-toned fabric
3yd × 36in light-toned fabric
Lining to fit

Cutting guide
468 diamonds in dark-toned fabric (template 1)
468 diamonds in medium-toned fabric (template 1)
481 diamonds in light-toned fabric (template 1)
Note: half diamonds at the sides are counted as whole.

To make
Sew the shapes together, one dark, one medium and one light, as shown, to form blocks. Sew the blocks in the sequence shown. Piece by hand.

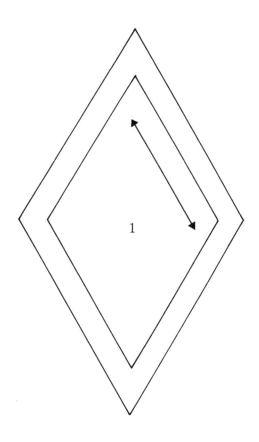

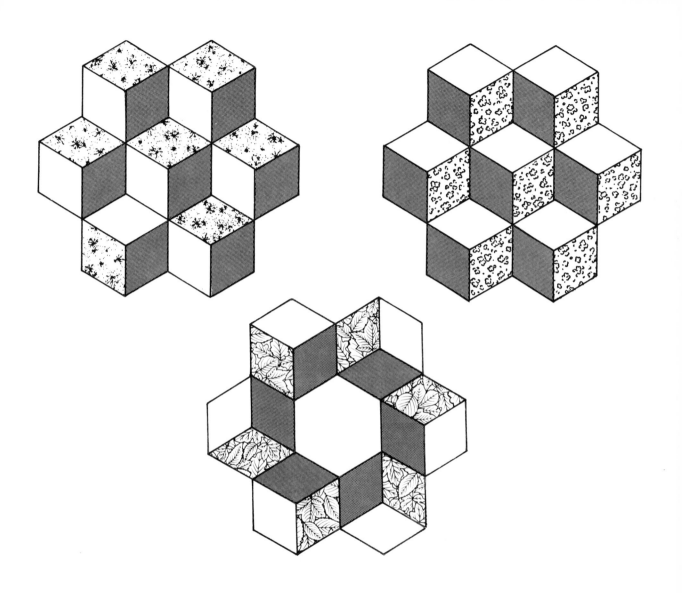

Some examples of how you can put
together light- and dark-toned fabrics
to create different effects.

'GRANDMOTHER'S GARDEN'

Cotton patchwork curtain or small quilt
English: third quarter of the 19th century
Length 100in × 72in

A patchwork panel of repeating cotton rosettes on a white ground. This composition is known as 'Grandmother's Garden' and the patchwork is one of five Museum examples which use rosettes of hexagons as the main design motif. The panel is unbordered and as the intended focal point of red rosettes is not placed centrally this may indicate that the piece was cut down from a larger patchwork or made from an unfinished, full-sized bed cover.

Both the patterned and white areas are made from hexagons of the same size and a number of different white and cream coloured fabrics are used in the ground. These include bleached calico, glazed cotton and figured cotton damask. The patterned areas show numerous small patterned dress fabrics of cotton and finely woven wool with some grey flannel shirt fabrics included. Most of the fabrics date from the middle of the 19th century whereas some large scale floral designs date from the late 1860s.

There is no evidence that the patchwork is interlined and the white cotton lining is a later addition, possibly dating from the reconstruction of the patchwork. The lining is attached to the patchwork top with functional quilting of vertical and horizontal lines which has given the surface a ridged appearance.

Given by Colonel G. Morphew   (Museum no. Circ. 94–1934)

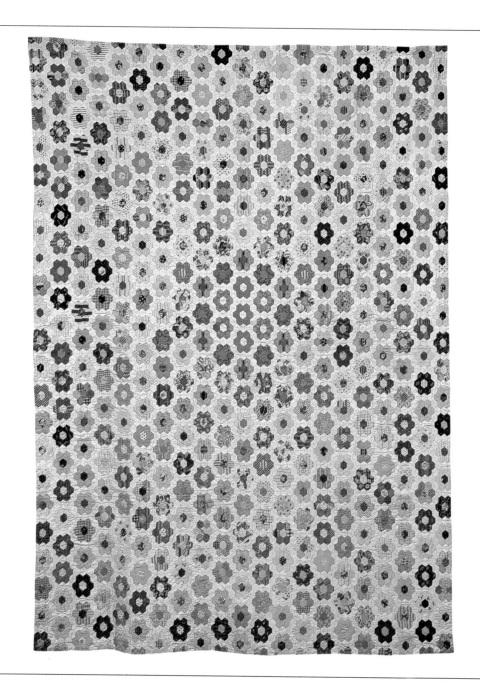

INSTRUCTIONS

This bed cover is made in ¾in hexagons in dark-toned and patterned fabrics on a cream background. There is no border.

Each rosette consists of seven patterned hexagons, and each coloured rosette is surrounded by 12 cream hexagons. Colours chosen will depend on availability of fabric, but have been given here in terms of pattern and cream.

There are 453 complete, or nearly complete, rosettes. The quilt is lined but is unquilted.

Instructions for sewing hexagons are given on page 15.

Materials

9yd × 36in different patterned fabrics
9yd × 36in cream-coloured fabric
Lining to fit

Cutting guide

Cut as many patterned shapes as you need from template 1 to make three or four rosettes at a time until you have a total of 453.

To make

Sew together the rosettes, each surrounded by cream hexagons, as in the photograph. Remove papers and press well.

Sew the patchwork top to the lining, catching it at intervals to prevent the quilt 'ballooning'. All the piecing should be done by hand.

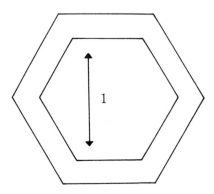

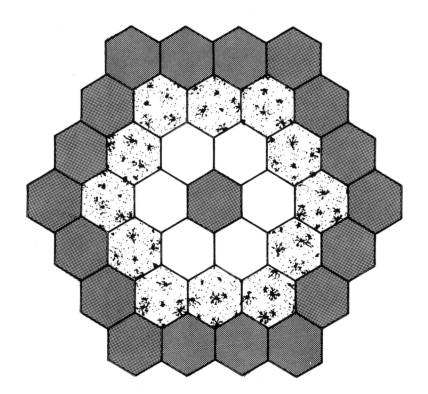

Some examples of different ways of sewing together hexagons.

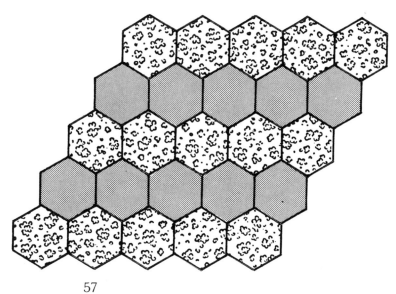

SILK QUILT

Silk patchwork quilt
English: third quarter of the 19th century
Length 90in × 86in

This is the only patchwork made of plain fabrics to be represented in this book. The design of the quilt mixes early and late traditions, with a formal, framed centre made of repeating six-point stars arranged concentrically to form hexagons and squares.

The use of plain silk dress fabrics for this quilt has provided a design of vibrant contrasting colours, with surprising combinations such as bright blue and brown which are rather more reminiscent of American Amish quilting than of English work. However, the colours used provide a perfect display of fashionable British taste in the third quarter of the 19th century.

The quilt is interlined and backed with pale brown cotton and is quilted with a trellis design in brown cotton. The use of a large variety of dress silks and the skillful, yet serviceable, quilting pattern suggests that this quilt could have been made by a fashionable dressmaker.

Given by Miss Tomes   (Museum no. T.76–1937)

INSTRUCTIONS

Much of the success of this sumptuous quilt in glowing silks depends on the clever arrangement of the colours. The shapes used are: a 1½in diamond, a 1½in hexagon, a triangle with a 6½in base and a trapezoid to fill in the edges. There is a 13in border, quilted in diamond shapes, and there is quilting round some of the others.

Although the photographed quilt measures 90in × 86in making it using the following templates will give you a square quilt of 86in × 86in. The diamonds are arranged as stars. They are separated by hexagons and six of the stars are made of 1in diamonds edged with red.

The quilt could be made in cottons instead of silks, though the brilliance of the colours might be lost.

Materials

27in × 36in varied cream fabrics (stars)
18in × 36in burgundy fabric (hexagons)
18in × 36in pale grey fabric
Scraps of dark red and orange fabric (hexagons)
18in × 18in dark grey fabric (central hexagons)
36in × 36in blue fabric (stars and triangles)
45in × 36in black fabric (hexagons and edges)
42in × 36in red fabric (diamonds and edging strips)
36in × 36in varied green fabrics
18in × 36in pale grey fabric (outer hexagons)
36in × 36in varied brown fabrics (hexagons)
27in × 36in pale mauve fabric (stars)
27in × 36in dark mauve fabric (stars)
6yd × 36in brown border fabric
Lining and wadding to fit

Cutting guide

42 diamonds in cream fabric (template 1)
7 18 × ½in edging strips *(NB: add seam allowance)* in red
36 hexagons in burgundy fabric (template 2)
84 diamonds in pale grey fabric (template 3)
3 hexagons in red fabric (template 2)
3 hexagons in orange fabric (template 2)
12 hexagons in dark grey fabric (template 2)
72 diamonds in blue fabric (template 3)
23 hexagons in burgundy (template 2)
7 hexagons in rust (template 2)

108 diamonds in varied cream fabrics (template 3)
66 hexagons in black fabric (template 2)
168 diamonds in varied green and dark blue fabrics (template 3)
206 diamonds in red fabric (template 3)
52 hexagons in pale grey fabric (template 2)
102 diamonds in dark mauve fabric (template 3)
102 diamonds in light mauve fabric (template 3)
98 hexagons in varied brown fabrics (template 2)
46 part hexagons in black fabric (template 2)
28 edging shapes in black fabric (template 4)
36 triangles in blue fabric (template 5)
32 triangles in brown border fabric (template 5)
4 corner triangles in brown border fabric (template 6)
2 border strips 91in × 13in
2 border strips 63in × 13in

To make

Work from the centre outwards, piecing stars and hexagons in the colours shown in the photograph.

Quilt the border in diagonals, and the main part along the edges of the patches. All this piecing should be done by hand.

All these templates are ½ size.

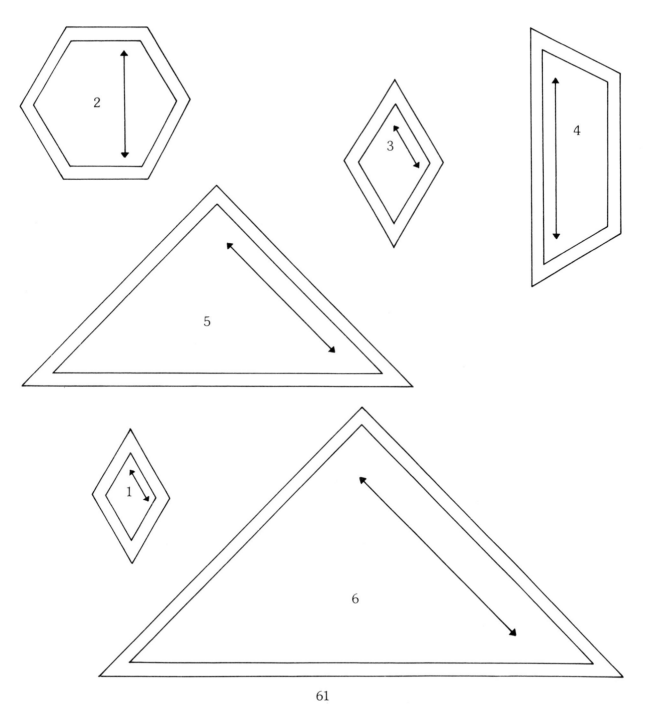

'STAR' QUILT

Cotton patchwork quilt
American: late 19th century
Length 92in × 92in

This is one of four American patchworks in the Museum's collection. The design shows a large single star which is constructed from concentric circles of equal-sized diamonds of printed cottons. The star is surrounded by a rust-coloured fabric which has a small-scale, printed design.

The quilt relies on the choice of small patterned printed cottons for the boldness and clarity of its design. Stripes, dots and variations of other simple repeating designs are used. The only floral design in the quilt, a flamboyant navy blue and white *art nouveau* design, is also the easiest to date and suggests that the quilt was made at the end of the 19th century.

American patchwork designs showing large central stars have been given various names in the past and, as well as 'Rising Star', 'Star of Bethlehem' and 'Lone Star', these have also been known as 'Blazing Star' and, more regionally, 'Lone Star of Texas'. Although complete, this bed cover does not have an outer border. On other examples this usually takes the form of squares or stripes of plain or patterned fabrics. Despite its association with America, large star designs are not exclusive to that country as British examples have been traced back as far as the late 18th century.

The quilt is interlined and lined with brown printed cotton. It is quilted in a simple linear design which follows the direction of the patchwork diamonds.

Given by Mrs Foster Stearns   (Museum no. T.99–1936)

INSTRUCTIONS

When this lovely quilt is made up using the following instructions it will measure 90in × 90in, rather than the photographed quilt's dimensions of 92in × 92in. It is made up of 3in diamonds in six colours, light tones graduating to dark tones, radiating from a central yellow eight-diamond star. Filling the space between the eight points of the star are four 27in corner squares and four triangles, all in rust colour. The triangles measure 36in across the base, with 27in sides.

The quilt is bound with long bias strips of another fabric, similar in tone and colour to the squares and triangles but slightly different in pattern.

Each diamond is outlined in quilting stitches which continue in parallel lines right up to the edges.

Such a quilt could be copied in modern fabrics, though diamonds are not the easiest shapes to sew because of their sharp points, and because their sides tend to stretch. Instructions for sewing diamonds are given on page 15.

Materials

72in × 36in yellow fabric
72in × 36in pale pink fabric
81in × 36in dark pink striped fabric (but add more if stripes are to go in same direction)
72in × 36in blue spotted fabric
72in × 36in navy blue flowered fabric
72in × 36in grey fabric
5yd × 36in rust fabric
Bias binding to tone
Wadding and lining to fit

Cutting guide

104 diamonds in yellow fabric; 8 for the centre of the star, 56 for the second yellow ring and 40 for the points of the star.

112 diamonds in pink fabric, 16 for the first ring round the centre star, 64 for the second ring and 32 for the points of the star.

120 diamonds in dark pink striped fabric; 24 for the first ring, 72 for the second ring and 24 for the points of the star.

112 diamonds in blue spotted fabric; 32 for the first ring, 64 for the first repeat of each star 'leg' and 16 for the points of the star.

104 diamonds in navy blue flowered fabric; 40 for the first ring, 56 for the second repeat of each star leg and eight for the points of the star

96 diamonds in grey fabric; 48 for the first ring, and 48 for the star legs (*There are no final grey diamonds in each point*) Note: Total number of diamonds: 648

4 $27\frac{1}{2}$in squares in rust coloured fabric (*$\frac{1}{4}$in seam allowance included*)

4 triangles, base 36in, sides 27in in rust coloured fabric (the template should be drawn out to these measurements and the $\frac{1}{4}$in seam allowance added afterwards).

To make

Sew the diamonds and build up the star from the centre to the outside in colours shown. Join the squares and triangles to the star. Remove papers and press well.

When quilting patchwork of this size, a large quilting frame is recommended. However, if the three layers are tacked together securely and the surplus quilt is rolled, it is possible to work at a table. Piece by hand.

'DOUBLE NINE-PATCH'

Cotton patchwork quilt
American: late 19th century
Length 88in × 72in

This quilt has a repeating design of plain white and mustard yellow and white checked cotton in which pattern blocks of five units of five squares of coloured fabric alternate with plain white cotton squares. The maker, Mrs Margaret Whitacre of Montpelier, Indiana, has added further interest to the quilt with repeating blocks of very fine quilting showing a design of overlapping wine glass circles.

The tradition of naming quilts is peculiar to America, although in recent years this practice has also been spreading to Britain. This particular pattern has at least three different titles: 'Double Nine-Patch', describes the number and arrangement of the patterned squares used in the design, whereas 'Puss in the Corner' and 'Burgoyne's Surrender' have their origins in social and military history. The quilt is interlined, although this has been flattened through use, and is lined with coarse white cotton fabric.

Given by Mrs A. Leese   (Museum no. T.154–1979)

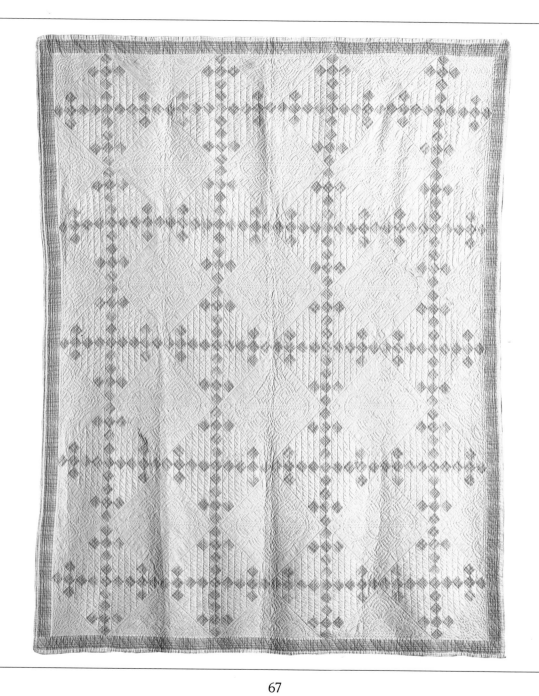

INSTRUCTIONS

A pleasing design of double nine-patch blocks alternating with richly-quilted white squares makes this an attractive and unusual bed cover. The yellow and white nine-patch blocks are also quilted, but this time in straight lines.

The quilt has 32 complete 12in squares, 20 of which are pieced, 14 half squares and 4 quarter squares. The squares are set on the diagonal.

The pieced 12in squares are made up of 4 4in plain white squares and 5 4in gingham and white squares. The latter are composed of four $1\frac{1}{3}$in white squares and five $1\frac{1}{3}$in yellow gingham squares. There is a $1\frac{1}{2}$in border in yellow gingham and a plain $\frac{1}{2}$in binding.

Materials

8yd × 36in white fabric
3yd × 36in yellow gingham fabric
Wadding and lining to fit

Cutting guide

12 $12\frac{1}{2}$in squares in white fabric
14 half $12\frac{1}{2}$in squares in white fabric (*add further seam allowance at the long edge*)
4 quarter $12\frac{1}{2}$in squares in white fabric (*add further seam allowance at the two short edges*)
80 5in squares in white fabric
400 squares in white fabric (template 1)
500 squares in yellow fabric (template 1)
2 $2\frac{1}{2}$in strips, 73in long in yellow gingham fabric
2 $2\frac{1}{2}$in strips, 87in long in yellow gingham fabric
Strips of white fabric for binding

To make

Cut all squares as given above. Seam allowances have been included except where stated. Piece the small squares first, sewing together two coloured and one plain square in a strip, then one coloured and two plain squares, then two coloured and one plain. Join these three strips to make squares.

Make the large patterned squares in the same way using the pieced squares and the 5in plain squares.

Join the resulting pieced and plain squares in strips to form the quilt. Quilt the pieced squares diagonally, and quilt the plain squares following the diagram given. Add the yellow gingham border, quilting it diagonally. Bind the quilt with strips of cream coloured fabric.

This quilt can be pieced by hand and machine.

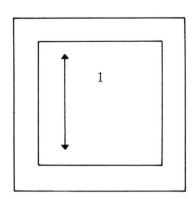

A quilting example.

AVERIL COLBY CUSHIONS

Cotton patchwork chair seat and back pad
English: 1953
Seat 15in × 12½in × 1¾in
Back Pad 13½in × 7in

Two patchwork cushions worked in white, grey and black printed cottons. The chair seat uses one black, three plain grey, and four black and white patterned prints (including a polka dot) and these have been carefully selected and cut to create a secondary pattern to the main patchwork design. The sides of the chair seat and back pad are both patched in a chequerboard of ½in black and white cotton squares and both are lined with scarlet coloured glazed cotton. There are seat ties and back flaps on the cushions to secure them to a chair.

The seat is padded with foam and the pad with capok.

Both pieces were designed and hand sewn by Averil Colby, the textile historian, and the seat cushion was used as a pattern in the Needlework Development Scheme's book *And So To Embroider* (1959), illustrated on an upright, white wooden kitchen chair.

The Needlework Development Scheme, which ran from 1934 to 1961, was founded with the stated aims of improving the standard of domestic embroidery. Loan exhibitions of historical and modern embroideries were organized, and with the assistance of many leading designers and craftsworkers the Scheme published a series of books illustrating the work of contemporary embroiderers. The Museum owns one other patchwork cushion cover designed by Averil Colby based on her very authoritative knowledge of the patterns and technique of historic patchwork.

Given by The Needlework Development Scheme

(Museum no. Circ. 273&A–1962)

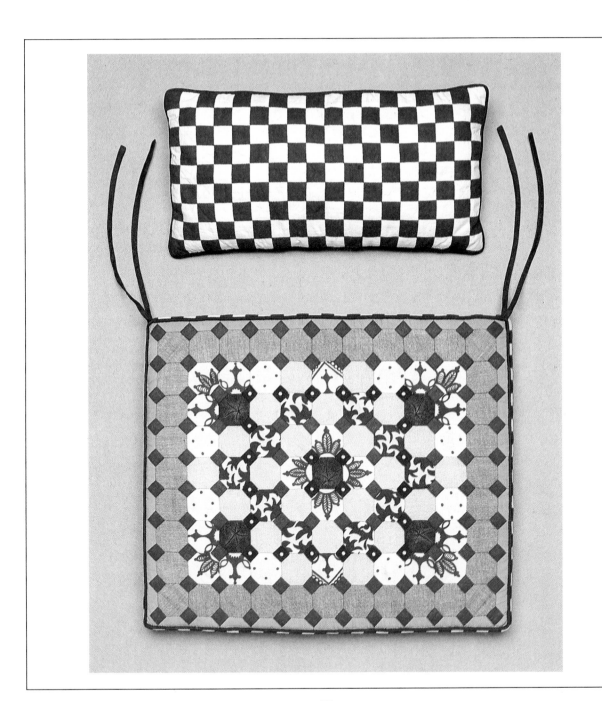

INSTRUCTIONS

This lovely seat cover with matching cushion has a subtle design of octagons and squares in grey, black and white. Each colour makes its own pattern while forming the overall pattern, like a fugue in a piece of music.

The octagons are $1\frac{1}{4}$in across and their linking black squares are $\frac{1}{2}$in, as are the squares on the seat gusset. There is an outer 'frame' of $1\frac{1}{2}$ rows of grey octagons and black squares inside which is a rectangle of carefully chosen and matched black and white patterned octagons, broken at regular intervals by plain grey octagons. Note how the plain octagons are placed, carrying their subsidiary theme among the patterned areas, and how the patterned octagons make their own perfectly balanced design. At the centre is a black octagon surrounded by four matching and patterned octagons to complete this satisfying design. Study it carefully before choosing fabrics.

The back pad is a black and white chequerboard patchwork of $\frac{3}{4}$in squares.

Materials

9in × 36in grey fabric
18in × 36in black fabric
18in × 36in white fabric
9in × 36in patterned fabric (*the amount depends on pattern matching*)
4yd of piping cord
Black bias binding
Padding and lining to fit

Cutting guide

Cushion top
36 grey octagons (template 1)
36 grey half octagons (template 2)
22 plain octagons (template 1)
5 black octagons (template 1)
36 patterned octagons (4 for central motif) (template 1)
96 squares in black fabric (template 3)
Gusset
106 black squares (template 3)
106 white squares (template 3)
Back pad
81 $1\frac{1}{4}$in squares in black fabric for back pad
81 $1\frac{1}{4}$in squares in white fabric for back pad
red lining 16in × $13\frac{1}{2}$in
red lining $14\frac{1}{2}$in × 8in

To make

Form the central motif first, sewing together one black and four patterned octagons. Continue to piece from the centre outwards, referring to the photograph and placing the patterns so that they match. Make up the gusset from two rows of alternating black and white squares.

When complete, cover the piping cord with bias binding. Baste and stitch it in position round the seat. Pad and line the seat and the pad.

All piecing should be done by hand.

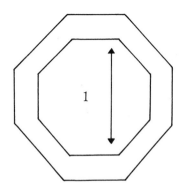
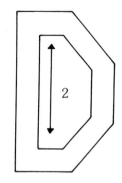
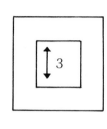